WARTON & FRECKLETON RECALLED

by
PETER BENSON
(Chairman, Warton History Society)

LANDY PUBLISHING
1995

ISBN 1 872895 25 5

Landy Publishing have also published:
'Blackpool & The Fylde Past & Present' by Alex Maitland & Bernard Drinkall
'Blackpool & Fleetwood A Century Ago' by Bob Dobson
'Preston Past and Present' by Stephen Sartin
'Preston A Century Ago' by Stephen Sartin
'Fresh Air & Fun; a Blackpool Miscellany' edited by Bob Dobson
'In Lancashire Language; Lancashire Dialect Verse' edited by Bob Dobson
. . . and other books on Lancashire history and dialect. Full details from Landy Publishing, 'Acorns', 3 Staining Rise, Staining, Blackpool FY3 OBU Tel/Fax 01253 886103

Printed by Turner & Earnshaw Limited, Westway House, Sycamore Avenue, Burnley, Lancashire.

PREFACE

At long last, the Warton History Society has got down to achieving one of the objects that was stated when it was founded twenty five years ago as 'Project 70'. That was to produce a written 'History of Warton'. This book is a start towards that object. It mainly contains photographs, all of some historical interest, and as much information as we have been able to gather about them. We have widened the scope to include Freckleton, as the two villages are closely linked. Indeed, to many who pass through, they appear to form one unit.

Many hours have been spent putting this book together, and I must make it quite clear that it has been a team effort. On behalf of the Society, I express thanks to the staff at the local libraries, to the editor of the 'Lytham St Annes Express', to Bob Dobson for his help on the publishing side, to Harry Robinson, and especially to the rest of the team: Rowena Derbyshire, Tom Doughty and Roy Hargreaves for collecting the photographs and writing the captions. We express our gratitude to all those who have loaned photos and allowed us to use them. These are acknowledged alongside the photos, as appropriate. Where no acknowledgement is made, it means that the photo has come from the Society's collection, as also have the cuttings and old adverts.

Inevitably in any book, mistakes can be made and I ask for forgiveness if this is found to be the case. Please bring any such mistakes to the attention of the Society's committee. Furthermore, if anyone has any photos of Warton and Freckleton, or has any information of any kind about the buildings, the inhabitants, or ANYTHING about this piece of Lancashire, we will be pleased and grateful for that information, as we are hoping to embark on a much more detailed 'history' as soon as time permits.

Lastly, the publishing team have asked that thanks be expressed to my wife Mary for providing innumerable cups of coffee and pieces of cake.

Peter Benson, Chairman Warton History Society.

Moorhead, 61 Harbour Lane, Warton, Preston.
Telephone 01772 632252

Project '70 begins to trace Fylde history

PROJECT 70 — the recently - formed organisation dedicated to the task of tracing a history of South Fylde —has begun work.

Tomorrow night, they are holding their second meeting at the parish rooms, Warton, when Mr

Adrian Murphy talks about windmills of the Fylde.

The meeting will be the first at which members will be "signed on." It is estimated about 60 amateur historians will join.

A committee has already been formed and has started plotting the future of "Project 70."

The society is the brainchild of Mr Roy Hargreaves, of Canberra-way, Warton.

He told me: "We are making an impact. People are becoming interested in what we are trying to do."

During the summer, it is hoped to organise trips to places of interest in the Fylde with local experts to act as guides.

The committee has already begun work on recording interviews with elderly local residents to capture permanently their descriptions of the South Fylde at the turn of the century.

"We have held two interviews and have more planned," said Mr Hargreaves, who added, "but two elderly residents, with whom we had arranged to hold interviews, died shortly before we could record their memories."

How the Lytham St. Annes Express helped to publicise the society in 1969.

In 1912 Mr and Mrs Richard Bickerstaffe posed to have their photograph taken outside their home, 'School Farm' in Bank Lane.

They had previously lived in 'Primrose Cottage' which was further along Bank Lane.

As the name suggests, the farm was owned by Warton Endowed School, the rent helping with the running cost of the school.

Along with a large number of other properties, 'School Farm' was requisitioned in 1940 by the Air Ministry when Warton Aerodrome was being built. At the end of the war the School were unable to afford the price asked, and so they could not resume ownership.

(B. Bickerstaffe)

4

6. **Warton** (on the Ribble, E. of Lytham; v.): *Wartun* DB, *Wartuna* 1153-60 Ch (orig.), *Warton* 1227 LF, 1332 LS, etc. Probably O.E. *weard-tūn (cf. *weard-seld* " guard-house," etc., G. *Wartburg*). This etymology seems fairly certain for Warton in Lonsdale, and plausible for Warton in Am. Warton Bank would be suitable as a lookout place; the ground W. of Warton along the Ribble is very low and was in old days mostly uninhabitable. O.E. *waroþ* (*wearþ*) " shore " is also possible as first el., but a name " shore town " is not very distinctive, as several old villages are on the shore.

Cowburn or **Cowburgh** (old estate): *Couburugh* 1189-94 Ch (in ChR 1336), *Cuburne, insula de Cuburc* (*Kuburne*) a 1246 CC. The original name was probably *Cū-burne* " cow brook," *-burgh* being due to a deliberate change.

7. **Bryning with Kellamergh** (N.E. of Lytham).

Bryning (h.): *Birstaf brinn[ing]* 1201 LPR, *Birstatbrunning* 1236 LI, *Burstad Brining* 1243 LI, *Burwadbruning* 1249 IPM; *Brunigg'* 1252 IPM, *Brining, Brunigge* 1254 IPM, *Brining* 1341 IN, etc., *Brinȳge* 1332 LS, *Brynin'* Waugh. The name has a curious history. In the earliest sources it is a double-barrelled name. From about 1250 the first part is dropped. I explain the first part as an O.N. *Bjárstaðr* (whence Norw. Bjaastad, Bjastad) meaning " farmstead "; *Bjár-* is the gen. of *býr* (cf. E. *byrlaw<býjarlǫg*); *staðr* means " place." The same name is Birstwith, W. Yks.: *Birstad* 13 cent. The second el. may be the O.E. pers. n. *Bryning* or O.Swed., O.Dan. *Bryning*. Or it may be an earlier name of the place, e.g., an O.E. patronymic *Bryningas*. I suppose Byrstath Bryning means Bryning Farm. The order between the elements is due to Celtic influence. A Celtic el. is found in the next name.

Kellamergh (h.): *Kelfgrimeshereg* 1201 LPR, *Kelgrimesarge* a 1246 CC, *Kelgrimisarhe* 1236 LI, *Kelghgrymeshare* 1285 LAR, *Kelgrimisharg* 1249 IPM, *Kelgrimeshar'* 1254 IPM, *Kelgrymessaregh* 1276 ClR, *Kelgrimeshargh* 1297 LI, *Kelgmesargh* 1332 LS, *Kilgrymesargh* 1347 LF, *Kellamoor* Waugh. The " ergh, or shieling, of *Kelgrim." On *ergh, argh* see p. 10. *Kelgrim* is a Scand. pers. n., derived by Björkman, Namenkunde, from O.N. *Ketilgrimr. Yet the earliest form does not quite bear out this suggestion.

The village's names explained by Professor Ekwall in his book *'The Place - Names of Lancashire'* (1922). The smaller extracts are from a national gazetter of the same year.

5. **Freckleton** (on the Ribble; W. of Newton; v.): *Frecheltun* DB, *Frecheltuna* 1153-60 Ch (orig.), *Frekiltona, ffrekelton* c 1190 CC, *Frekelton* 1202, 1227 LF, etc., *ffrekilton* 1332 LS, *Frekilton* 1428 LF; *Freketon* 1201 LPR; *Frekenton* 1201f. LPR, 1270 LAR; *Frequinton* 1202f. LPR, *Frequenton* 1204 LPR; *Frekintone* 1212 RB; *Frequelton* 1212 LI; *de Frikelton* 1246 LAR. S. of the vil. is a point of land called the Naze: " the famous Neb of the Nese," 1771 Whitaker, Hist. of Manchester I. 129. In Whitaker's time the Ribble formed a large bend here. The depth was 15ft.

This is a very difficult name, to no small extent owing to the variety in the early forms. The forms in *l* (*Frekelton*, etc.) are obviously to be preferred to those in *n* (*Frekenton*, etc.), as they are more common and evidenced earlier. No doubt *n* is due to Norman dissimilation. Then there is the question if the spellings with *qu* for *k* (*Frequelton, Frequinton*) are worthy of attention. I suppose they indicate that a *w* has been lost after *k*. Sephton assumes as first el. O.E. *Frecwulf*, but such a name is not evidenced; the instance in Searle is Frankish. If the form contained a *w*, I think the first el. is an O.E. *Frecwāl containing O.E. *frec* " greedy " or " dangerous " (cf. Förster, E. St. 39, 328 ff.) and O.E. *wāl* " pool," referring to the deep place in the river mentioned. This seems to me the most probable explanation. If the original form had no *w*, it is perhaps an *l*-derivative of the stem in O.E. *frec, fræc*. This may be an O.E. *Freca pers. n. (cf. *Freca*) or a derivative of the O.E. adj. *frēcel* (M.E. *frekel*) " wicked: dangerous " (cf. Förster *l.c.*), a name of the pool.

The type of cart shown here was a familiar sight on the lanes of Warton and Freckleton. Usually piled high with hay. The waggoner walking alongside. ready to apply the brakes when the horse took it into its head to wander off.

Here Mr Hankinson proudly stands with loaded waggon at Balderstone Mill.

How Freckleton was described in the 1895 edition of Barrett's Directory of Preston & District.

FRECKLETON.

This township has a large village, pleasantly situated on the north bank of the Ribble, 2¼ miles south from Kirkham, and 8 miles west from Preston. It is in the Blackpool parliamentary division, and in the Fylde county council division and Union. The parish council consists of nine members. *Holy Trinity Church* was erected in 1837. It is a plain brick edifice in the Perpendicular style, and consists of nave and chancel, with a western tower and small spire containing one bell. The east window of stained glass is to the memory of the late Mrs. Myres. Another stained window is to the memory of Mr. Green. There are 230 sittings, 150 of which are free. The benefice is a vicarage of the annual value of £160, in the patronage of the Dean and Canons of Christ Church, Oxford. Rev. Edward John Hack, vicar. The old *Wesleyan Chapel*, erected in 1840, has been replaced by a very neat edifice, built at a cost of £1,400, on the site of the old building. There is sitting accommodation for 300 persons. The *Primitive Methodists'* new chapel is a neat Gothic building of patent brick, with stone dressings, having a graceful spire. It was designed by Messrs. Mould, of Manchester, and the contractor was Mr. John Gardner, of Kirkham. It will seat 266 persons, and the cost of erection was £1,200. The old chapel has been converted into a school. In the village is a *Friends' Meeting House*. A cotton mill gives employment to a considerable number of people. The township contains 2,417 acres, and the rateable value is £6,480. The population in 1851 was 968; 1861, 879; 1871, 930; 1881, 1,134; and 1891, 1,306.

PARISH COUNCIL.—Richard Cookson (chairman), Richard Mason, John Cartmell, William D. Butler, Benjamin E. Jones, John Whiteside, John T. Rigby, James Iddon, Thomas Rawcliffe. *Rural District Councillor,* John Kirby.

Post and Money Order Office at Mrs. Ann Spencer's. Letters arrive from Preston, *via* Kirkham, at 7 a.m., and are despatched at 4 p.m.

Three views of Warton Aerodrome; two wartime scenes and a later one. The view looking over the Airfield with the hangers in the foreground shows four-engined 'Liberator' Bombers and single-engined 'Mustang' Fighters. During 1944, 2,204 'Liberators' and 3,227 'Mustangs' passed through Warton for modification or repair. Other types of aircraft brought the yearly total to nearly 7,000.

The Operations Room shown in the middle photograph was centre of all the comings and goings of Base Air Depot No 2 (BAD 2). The 310th Ferry Squadron was based at Warton from November 1943. In its first full month of operation, the Squadron delivered 1,243 aircraft including 627 Bombers and 554 Fighters.

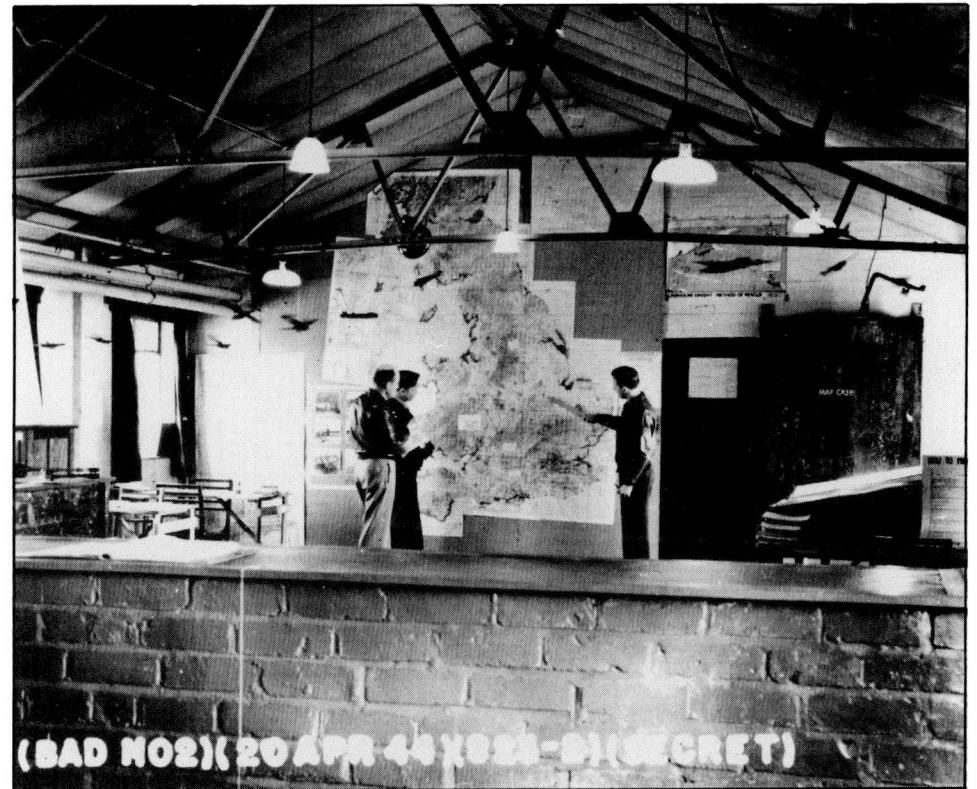

The third view looks to the North over the hangers to the village and beyond. Taken in 1970 the photograph shows Beech and Poplar Avenues, but Ash Drive between Poplar Ave. and Church Road is an unmade road, with no houses between Lytham Road and Blenheim Drive.

(British Aerospace Archive)

The Engine Overhaul Department was set up at the end of 1943 working on radial engines for the *'Liberator'* Bombers. By January 1944, all work was concentrated on servicing the Allison (V1710) and the Packard Rolls (V1650) inline-engines for the *'P 38 Lightning'* and the *'P 51 Mustang'* fighters. It may be remembered that the installation of the Packard-Built *'Rolls Royce Merlin'* changed the *'Mustang'* from a moderate aeroplane to one of the very best long range Escort Fighters of the war.

The view over the hangers shows a line up of 17 *'Mustangs'* and one *'Lightning'*. It was to be many years before the English Electric version of the *'Lightning'* would be seen on the same tarmac.

(British Aerospace Archive)

Early Educationists believed that a healthy body and a healthy mind went together. Here a class from Warton School are ready to 'enjoy' their P.T. lesson. The little girl at the left in the front row is Ellen (Nellie) Lee who went on to achieve fame as Warton's first Cotton Queen in 1932.

(Mrs R. Derbyshire)

The class of 1913 photographed with Headmaster Mr Lockey outside the School main entrance. This door is now blocked and hidden within the extensions that were carried out in 1965/6. Nellie Lee is again in the front row this time wearing white bows, third from the left. Annie Fisher is at the left hand end of the same row.

(Mrs R. Derbyshire)

Warton School. This teacher's name isn't known, though she became Mrs Heaton and lived in Freckleton.

It is unlikely that there would be twentynine children of such an age range in one class, so perhaps this group is the whole of the Junior School. It was taken in the School yard - see the playground ladder in the background - about 1920.

(Mrs A. Kay)

Warton Sunday School with Dr. Stewart Lawton. The teachers at the rear are Miss Dugdale, Mr Swarbrick, Mrs Lawton, Nellie Lee and Irene Richardson. The photo was taken in 1955.

(Mrs R. Derbyshire)

10

Warton School in the early 1930's with Mr Seed at the rear of the class.

This classroom is now part of the school hall. The wood and glass partition could be folded back to make a larger room. It was in the corner of the other class that the school stage was erected by the Warton drama group when it was needed.

(Mrs Gornall)

Mrs A Sumner with her baby Mary outside the gate of Blackfield End Farm, Church Road, Warton. This farmhouse is still standing and is occupied by the Winstanleys, who farm the land. Little Mary became Mrs Ernest Barlow, and they later farmed Sykes Hall Farm, next door to Blackfield End. Mary is still alive and well as I write, about to celebrate her ninetieth birthday.

(Mrs B. Sidebottom)

Miss Dugdale's class in Warton School, probably 1929.

These were the infants, lined up with Miss Dugdale are back row (left to right) Bobbie Shorrock, A.N. other, Dick Townsend, John Proctor, Leslie Thompson and Cyril Helm.

In the centre row: Hilda and Ruby, (the Gardner twins) Annie Fenton, Margery Hogarth, Jessie Snape, and Rowena Townsend.

Front row: Doris Bonney, Sidney Hutchinson, and Marion Hodgson.

(Mrs R. Derbyshire)

The *'Clifton Arms'* used to have a thatched roof and a bowling green, the left hand end was a storage barn and only fairly recently was it converted to a restaurant. It is now called 'The Pickwick Tavern' and the bowling green is long gone.

The interior view shows the Clifton Arms prior to it being completely re-furbished about 1970. *'C & S Brewery'* was taken over by Bass & Co. in 1961.

(Mr R. Hargreaves)

Two views of the Clifton Arms. One taken in the early 30's shows the forecourt cobbled right down to the road. The area was used as a bus stop. The weighing machine was presumably to pass the time while waiting for the bus to Lytham.

The two cottages have since been demolished to make way for four flats. One of the cottages had been a Fish & Chip shop.

The 'C & S' Wines & Spirits so prominently advertised were 'Catterall and Swarbrick' the Blackpool brewers.

The sandstone kerb and guttering seems only to go as far as Harbour Lane.

In the earlier view of about 1910 the advertising refers only to 'teas and refreshments' 'picnic parties catered for'. This was an attempt to attract 'tea total' customers.

(Mr J.Plummer)

Copyright W.W.L. 16.   Main Road, Warton, (West Lancs).   Raphael Tuck & Sons London.

14

House boats on the foreshore to the East and West of the end of Guides Lane. The lane led from the river and joined Mill Lane and Highgate Lane. The houseboats were removed when the surrounding land was requisitioned when construction of the airfield commenced, although many had been destroyed in 1927 when the sea burst through and flooded large areas of the Fylde Coast.

A closer view of one of the boats with the family assembled, possibly for the weekend. Note that central heating is installed!

BOAT HOUSES WARTON

Guides House Warton.

Guides House Hotel Warton

The Cafe, Guides House Hotel Warton

View of *'The Guide's House'*, the pub at the river end of Guides Lane. *'Guide's House'* was originally the starting point for a walk across the river. It was the home of the guide who would take you across at low tide to Hesketh Bank.

When the training walls for the Port of Preston were built, crossing the river became impossible, a detour right into Preston was then needed.

The locals would bicycle to the pub but a landau service was operated from the main road, by Mr Wilson, who would take weekend visitors down the lane. He was always smartly dressed, complete with top hat and long whip.

A later view showing that by 1930 the visitors were arriving by *'Leyland Lion'* coaches on trips from Preston and beyond. The building had been extended at both the front and side.

The cafe and shop across the road from *'The Guide's House'* catering for the more sober visitors, offers included sweets and cigarettes at 5 for 2 pence.

16

Parish Council Meeting.

Elections for the Parish Council have usually taken place at the Assembly, but this practice would have been dispensed with this year even supposing the war had not put an end to rural electons. The reason is rather amusing. Elections for almost all Parish Councils are judged on a show of hands, but for the past 20 years there has almost invariably been a poll. So keen is your Freckletonian on local government matters that for nine seats there have been as many as 20 candidates, and after the annual meeting there was always somebody to get up and demand a poll.

Freckleton finally decided this was a farce and so made a petition to the County Authorities. The result was an order, dated August 3rd, 1939, cited as "The County of Lancaster (Township of Freckleton) Order, 1939," laying down that in future Parish Councillors shall be elected by nomination, and when the number of nominees exceeds the number of vacancies, by a poll.

* * *

Warton Meeting.

Warton Parish annual meeting will also take place in March, though the date has not yet been fixed.

Mr. Banks, Clerk to Freckleton Council, has been acting as Clerk to Warton and Bryning Council since September, when their Clerk, Mr. W. S. Buck, was called up. Mr. Buck, of Mount House, Freckleton, was, I imagine, an unusually young man to hold the position, but his grandfather was the late Mr. W. M. Buck, who held office before him for 30 years. Mr. W. S. Buck was a clerk in the Union Offices, Wesham.

* * *

One of the first plays presented by the Warton drama group was '9.45' the plays were performed in the school, what is now the hall, but was then three class rooms. The sliding screen between two of them was folded back and the third class - Miss Dugdale's room was used as a dressing room.

The cast was L to R:

Marion Fenton, James Kay, Doris Bonney, Jerry Buckley, Charlie Lister, Mary Richardson, Gerald Townsend, Mary Metcalf, Raymond Bickerstaff, Alfred Sumner, Jim Plummer
Seated: Arnold Shaw, Grace Hankinson, Snr, Tom Townsend, Grace Hankinson, Jnr, Albert Copeland.

(Mr. J. Plummer)

Warton St. Paul's has always been lucky to have a good choir. Here they pose for a celebration photograph.

Back row (L to R): John Braithwaite, Mr Edmundson, George Cook, A.E. Vickers, George Bamber, John Bonney and Albert Cook.

Middle row: Tom Townsend, Ruby and Hilda Gardner, Lizzie Bonney, Nora Smith, Marion Hodgson, Mary Smith, Edna Braithwaite, Jim Davidson.

Front row: Jimmy Miller, Ben Stevenson, Derek Townsend, Rueben Whiteside, Mason Rigby, Rev Halstead, Mrs Halstead, Stanley Fenton, John Bretherton, Gerald Townsend and Billy Rigby.

(Mr Rayton)

The 1968 Christmas party for Warton's pensioners, held in the Village Hall. Bonds of Elswick were the caterers responsible for the contented looks.

Prominent in the left foreground are (L to R) Mrs Baldwin, Miss Galloway and Kath Thompson, others include Mrs Mary Townsend and Miss Lee.

(Mrs R. Derbyshire)

Lime Tree House

The Old Vicarage, situated directly across the road from the Church, can still be seen. It is now approached via the cul-de-sac known as *'The Orchard'*. This view can now only be seen from the gardens of the houses on Lytham Road.

The last Vicar to live there was the Rev. Robert Halstead, who retired in 1952 after serving the village for 56 years.

His successor, The Rev. Dr. Lawton had the new vicarage built for him, and the old one was sold. Many of today's younger generation will remember it for the play group that was run there.

'Lime Tree House', further up Church Road on the left, has changed little over the years. It started life as a farmhouse; the outbuildings have been converted into houses.

For many years the end part of the barn was used by Jack Rigby to keep pigs in, and is still known to older villagers as *'The Piggery'*.

Warton Vicarage.

FRECKLETON INSTITUTE.

Two photographs of the same building, properly called *'The Hodgson Men's Institute'*. Mr Segar Hodgson was a great benefactor to Freckleton and to Kirkham, and in 1910 he gave this building and twenty six acres of land to Freckleton parish for the enjoyment of local folk. In accordance with his wishes, no intoxicants were allowed in the Institute.

The building was erected on the former *'Foldside Farm'*. Used as a Quaker Meeting House, and later in the 18th Century as a Methodist chapel for a while, in turn it became, after Hodgson's gift, the home of the parish council and women's Institute. It is said that, on quiet evenings, one can here the strains of *'Jerusalem'* when standing in or near the present village hall in School Lane. That's possibly because the hall stands on the site o'th' Institute.

One of a number of cottages on the East side of West End Lane. These buildings were typical Fylde cottages with thatched roofs and small windows.

The thatch was later replaced by corrugated iron sheeting, sometimes laid direct on the old thatch to deaden the noise of heavy rain beating on the roof. All these buildings have been demolished and replaced with modern houses. A later view appears on page 24. The lady is Emma Hogarth.

(Mrs M. Gornall)

'Straight Trees Farm' in Bank Lane is another old farm that has been converted to three dwellings. The lady standing in the doorway is Mrs Rachel Snape, holding her daughter Sheila. The two ladies on the road are Alice Snape and Mary Keenan. Mary worked with the Snape family on the farm.

Old Cottages, Freckleton

R. TOWNLEY
WARTON.

FAMILY GROCER,
TOBACCONIST, ETC.

Goods delivered. -:- Orders promptly attended to.

If there is a *'very centre'* of Freckleton - this is it. . We don't know when the village blacksmith's workshop, or *'Smithy'* was put up, but it is fairly certain that there was no planning permission for it, and that the first occupant was a *'squatter'* on common lands, as no deeds existed for it, Neverthless, it performed a useful purpose in the lives of villagers in the 17th and 18th Centuries. Notice the signpost directing travellers along the marsh road, which became Preston Old Road when the *'new'* road was constructed in 1927. The smithy was taken over by the District Bank, who built their bank, later to become the National Westminister Bank, on the site. The bank opened in 1913.

These thatched cottages, so typical of the Fylde, are thought to have been demolished to make room for the *'Plough Inn'* on Kirkham Road and for the making of Preston Road in the late years of the 19th century.
They had probably existed for 150 years.

'Crimble Cottage' at Bryning. Another of the area's cottages that once was thatched. This one has two floors. It stood at the top of Bryning Hill on the opposite corner to where the riding stables are today.

'Primrose Cottage' in Bank Lane with Mrs Richard Bickerstaffe and son William. This photograph was taken in 1910, just before the family moved to *'School Farm'* (see page 4). The cottage has since been modified but, unlike so many of Warton's old buildings, it is still in existence.

(Mr B. Bickerstaffe)

'Fletchers Farm' in Bank Lane: a recent view taken in 1994. This farm is now almost hidden from view behind 'Ferrier Bank' off Bank Lane. This row of bungalows was named after the great singer, Kathleen Ferrier, who for a while lived just across the road in 'Bank Lane.

Another view of John Hogarth's cottage in West End Lane (see page 21) with the thatching replaced and two new houses built right against the old building. These new houses were built in the 1970s, John's cottage has now gone but the line of the roof can still be seen on the wall of the new building.

Ruins, Peg Mill, Warton

Going · going · very nearly gone. Warton's peg mill was one of the very few in the area. Most being the more modern tower mills where the head automatically weather-cocked into wind.

With the peg mill, it had to be turned by the miller. which meant rotating the whole mill every time the wind changed.

This mill is very old, its true age is uncertain. It appears on Yates' map of 1786 but it was brought to Warton from Rufford, over the river, in 1717. Legend has it that the mill originally came from the fen district.

The peg still stands hidden behind the old building in Mill Lane just before the new houses.

25

Balderstone Mill's chimney overlooks some villagers in the early 1900's. The mill was erected by the Sowerbutts family in the 1800's is then passed to John Bibby & Sons before being bought by Messrs Birtwistle, the last owners. At its peak, the workforce operated 320 cotton weaving looms. 1980 brought closure and redundancy to the 50 workers. Demolition came soon afterwards, allowing houses to be built to accommodate the rapidly expanding population.

Here's Kirkham Road, Freckleton in the latter years of the 19th century. The photographer has caught the attention of a group of residents outside Whiteside's, a shop which sold almost everything villagers would need.

Notice the telegraph poles, a sure-fire way of 'dating' the glimpse of Freck's past life.

After the end of the war, the hangers at Warton were used as a training school to help enlisted men learn skills that would help them in civilian life when they returned to the United States. The airfield was handed back to the Royal Air Force in November 1945, and it was used as a storage area.

The English Electric Company became interested in using the site, and the first test flying at Warton by them was in August 1947.

By the early '50s most of the buildings had been taken over and renovation started.

This view of the main entrance shows the first name-plate. It is almost on the site of the present monolithic sign. Note that the traffic lights have not yet arrived and that 'C & S Ales' are still available at the Clifton Arms.

(British Aerospace Archive)

Church Road in the 1930s; the church wall on the right, and 'Rose Cottage' prominent on the left. The road in the left foreground led to the vicarage. The buildings seen have changed very little but the trees on the right were attacked by 'Dutch Elm' disease and many were felled. The ones on the left were attacked by 'new estate' disease, when the old vicarage grounds were sold and The Orchard was built.

(Mr J Plummer)

What an interesting skyline Freckleton used to have. Here's proof, two church steeples. The primitive Methodist Chapel, Preston Old Road, seen here, was brick built and cost £1,200 to build. The Holy Trinity Church of England church, first erected in 1839, enlarged in 1900, lost most of its steeple about 1980. This was originally built as a *chapel of ease* to Warton Church, dedicated to St Paul, which was originally built in 1724, and replaced with the present-day building in 1886.

Freckleton Club Day. Here, early on in the century, the proccession, which has a Sunday School look about it, is passing the Primitive Methodist Chapel in Preston Old Road. This was entirely separate from the Wesleyan Methodist Chapel, following the break, or one of the breaks, within the Methodist Church. The marshall seen in the centre may have been a Rechabite placed there to provide order and continuity to the procession. It is unlikely that safety would have been one of his considerations, as it is with today's marshalls. The fine chapel, also seen in the lower photos taken by Mr Hargreaves, a Kirkham photographer, was knocked down in the 1960's through being in a bad state of repair. The library now stands on the site. How long will that last? A group of houses is being built today (1995) on the left of the picture. Did the bike lying in the hedge belong to Mr Hargreaves?

Club day about 1920: the St Paul's Church group passing the fairground set up on what is now the Pickwick Tavern car park. (photographed from a similar position to the one seen on page 27).

The policeman was in attendance, but it is apparent that he is not so bothered in controlling traffic as he would be today. He's busy watching the 'A.A' Patrolman who's lost his motorcycle. This cross roads was for many years known as *Four Lane Ends*.

Freckleton's first woman Chairman

FOR the first time in their 69-year history, Freckleton Parish Council appointed a woman Chairman at their annual meeting in the Hodgson Institute last night.

She was Coun Miss Ruth Matthews, of Kirkham - road, Freckleton, who jointly held the honour of first Freckleton woman councillor when she joined five years ago with Coun Mrs S. Entwisle, who has now left the district.

Coun Miss Matthews obtained a Bachelor of Science degree at Liverpool University.

The retiring chairman, Coun J. P. Mayor, proposed Coun Miss Matthews, who was Vice-Chairman, and her election was seconded by Coun E. W. Hassall.

Coun Mayor thanked members and the Clerk, Mr W. S. Threlfall, for their support during the year, which had been one of progress.

GOOD EXAMPLE

Coun Miss Matthews commented that as first woman Chairman she would have to set a good example.

The council elected a retired local government officer, Coun Oscar Ridgard, of Kirkham-road, Freckleton, to be Vice-Chairman.

Coun Ridgard has been on the council for five years.

(1963 Lytham St. Annes Express)

The Club Day procession in Church Road, Warton. The route took the walkers as far as the *'Birley Arms'* where it turned round and re-traced the route. It has been stated that there was not a pause for refreshment. (or at least there wasn't an official one). The banner bearers and steerers had better watch where they are walking. There's been a horse on the road before them.

(Mr Rayton)

Freckleton Club Day · a similar shot, perhaps taken in the same year if fashions are compared. Certainly the two photos on this page were taken in the 1920's.

A special day in Freckleton's life. This gives a glimpse of the village and the villagers enjoying *'Club Day'* in the 1920's. The *'Cyclists Arms'* was a licensed puplic house on Lytham Road, near to where now stands *'The Plough'*, Cycling was a growth sport from the 1880's, and the name was chosen to attract business from the *'Wheelers'* who toured the Fylde's lanes, often in groups belonging to cycling clubs, or *'clarions'* as they were often known. It had previously been called *'The Tewitt Arms'* The *'club'* was the name given to the various Friendly Societies, often *'Rechabites'* or *'Mechanics'*, which were in existance locally and which held a procession to publicise themselves and the benefits of membership. Traditionally, the procession has long been held in June on a Saturday, though the early ones, from the 1840's were held on a March Monday. In the 1870's, churches began to participate in the event, a beano day on the villagers' calendar.

top left: Another year, another walk, this time photographed passing the parish room. The only way in was to use the external wooden stair.

The tall trees were in the grounds of the old vicarage and had a substantial rookery in the upper branches. Legend has it that when the aeroplanes came, the rooks went.

(Mrs M. Gornall)

below left: Warton Club Day 1938. The retiring Rose Queen was Miss Edith Scott and the newly crowned holder of the honour was Miss Marion Hodgson.

(Mrs R. Derbyshire)

below right: In 1939 Miss Hodgson is seen again, this time as the retiring Queen. As this was to be the last club day before the war, the newly elected Queen, Miss Doris Bonney was the last of the peace time Rose Queens. The ladies of the 'W.I.' made all the 'Roses'.

(Mrs R. Derbyshire)

Lytham Road Warton with Townsend's garage before the road was widened. The garage was one of the earliest buildings to have electricity in the village.

It is reported that when the Parish Council were discussing the installation of streetlights, one Councillor stated *'There's enough leets in Warton, trouble is they're all in Townsend's garage.'*

Lytham Road Warton looking towards Freckleton. The Post Office is clearly visible, with the Blacksmith's shop between it and the School. The School gable has on it a bell tower, which does not appear on later views.

(Mr Rayton)

Looking in the opposite direction but a few years later. Mill Lane is on the left. The tea room is at No 90 Lytham Road, and the church can be seen through the houses.

The bus is a *'Leyland Lion'* which was new to *'Ribble Buses'* in 1930. The bus drivers were friendly chaps who would stop wherever needed, and regular customers would be well looked after, even having the bus wait a while if they were a bit late coming down the lane.

(Mr J. Plummer)

These photos are linked to those of the old Freckleton cottages seen earlier. We are looking at Kirkham Road. Notice the *'mounting steps'*, (which were an aide to horse riders), outside the cottage, which got knocked down to make room for *'The Plough Inn'*, which is seen on the photo showing the bend in the road. See the Methodist Chapel in the background.

(Mrs A. Kay)

Bunker Street, Freckleton, showing the 'Ship Inn', in both background and in close-up. The street was snapped by Mr B. Hargreaves, a Kirkham professional photographer who recorded much of what he saw for posterity. He captured this scene about 1910. The street got its name from the fact that, at its end, coal was stored, as in a coal bunker, after being delivered by boat from across the Ribble and down the Douglas from Wigan. The 'Ship Inn' was one of Freck's eight pubs when there were only 900 inhabitants. There is a record of the pub being licensed in 1677, but it is thought to be the oldest Fylde inn, dating as far back as the 14th Century. The name reflects the village's maritime connections. Another pub close by was 'The Mariners Arms'.

opposite page: Part of the workforce of Balderstone Mill in the days before the First World War. The aprons being worn by the all-hatted team were called 'brats'. Notice they are nearly all wearing clogs, probably supplied and repaired by the village clogger at that time, Tom 'Clogger' Rawstrone.

Bill Fenton and Ted Dixon in the early 20's with their entry in the decorated pram race. They were probably photographed in Church Road.

(Mrs E Richardson)

Two views of Freckleton's busy hub. The upper one was probably taken at the village's celebrations for the coronation of King George the Fifth in 1911. See also the butcher's shop with its sunblind down. The butcher, Mr Bonney was probably keeping his eye on it from the celebrations.

The upper one shows the *Tewitt Arms* which later became known as the *Cyclists Arms*. More photos of this beerhouse are elsewhere in this book. A *tewitt* is a bird, also called a lapwing or a green plover.

Two views of Preston Road, Freckleton: The upper one looks from Naze Lane East, on the left, and shows a ropeworks or leather tanyard on the right. This is where today's Sports & Social Club stands. This postcard was posted to Master Joe Gardner in Liverpool by his Auntie staying in Freckleton in 1921. She tells him that the train from Liverpool arrived in Preston 17 minutes late, at 5.20pm, then she and Uncle Joe travelled to Kirkham on the 6.18pm, then *'by taxi to F., landed little different to 7pm'*

In the centre of the lower photo can be seen *'The Cyclists Arms'* also called *'The Tewitt Arms'* and the smithy, so it was taken before 1913, when that old building was replaced by a new bank. Shops today occupy the block on the left, and if you look very, very closely, you might see, just out of the camera's reach, the *'Coach & Horses'* pub, and maybe smell the beer.

Butcher Mr Bonney stands, about the turn of the century, in the doorway of the shop built in Kirkham Road by his butcher father, in 1864. At the same time he built the row of cottages it stands in (at the end of it actually). In 1948 the business passed from the Bonney family to their relatives the Snapes, when Tom Snape became the village butcher. His grandsons, John and Jim are *'pleased to meat'* villagers today. The shop next door on the photo became a front room for the Snape household about 1960 when the shop was run by Tom Snape Junior.

(Mrs P Mayland)

Here we see Harry Hall's cart loaded with coal which has almost certainly come by barge across the Ribble from Wigan. In the background Bunker Street can be seen. It is early on in the century. Harry had the contract for carting ash and *clinker* (cinders) from the mill to be used to repair the village's footpaths. There was a weighbridge for carts, and a separate one for motor wagons, or *lurries* as they were called, on which the weight of the load were measured. It is unlikely that they were over-worked.

There is some doubt about this view. The most likely explanation is that a flood repair was being effected to the banks of the Ribble at Freckleton. We know that such work was done in the early years of the century, and again after flooding in 1927. This photo was probably taken at the earlier time, when horse and man provided the power to get the job done.

Two views of Lytham Road, Freckleton. On the upper one, the Church of England School is seen on the left and there are children in the yard. Spot the church spire behind the trees. This was the scene of the 1944 disaster (see later photos), following which the school was repaired and used until the 1960's. Now, houses stand where children hopped and skipped. The motor lorry tells us that the photo was almost certainly taken in the 1930's.

On the lower shot, see Jack Hayes' hardware shop, small and recessed from the building line. Now this is occupied by the Co-op Chemists shop. The house on the right edge still stands. It was occupied until the 1970's by Jack Archer, who claimed to have been born in it, and that it was *next door to Warton Church*, By this he meant that there were no buildings between his house and the church at Warton, a mile away.

Balderstone Mill was possibly Lancashire's most Westerly cotton weaving mill. Here we see both some of the 320 looms on a day of celebration (a coronation perhaps) and its *'lodge'* where rainwater, some of it drained from the specially-designed roof with its North-facing *'lights'*, (windows) was held for use with the boilers, which made the steam for the engine which powered the machinery. It is likely that, from after the 1930's, the lodge would be unnecessary because each loom had its own electricity power source. The windows faced North because the daylight was steadier from there, not subject to the same variances as would be South-facing windows. On the site of Freckleton's *'satanic mill'* now stand Lodge Close, Mill View and Balderstone Road.

A line of the local children pose for the photographer outside Warton School. There was no need to worry about standing in the road; traffic was not what it is today. The school main entrance can be seen behind the railings.

The cottages and post office beyond have changed very little, but the houses on the left hand side were pulled down to widen the road. The lads in their cloth caps and white collars all look very smart.

Probably some of the same children at the bottom of Church Road. The church is seen through the trees on the right. This would not be a good place to stand and take a photograph today, not even with an instant point-and-shoot camera.

47

Freckleton cenotaph was erected to the memory of its fallen of the First World War in 1923. This Club Day Queen is paying her respects in 1930's, when many memories would be very fresh of those sixteen village lads who paid the supreme sacrifice. Lest we forget, their names were: Robert Banks, Henry Battersby, Ernest Cottam, Herbert Davies, John Eccles, John Robert Gregson, Joseph Halsall, Silvester Carr, Edward Ibbison, James Newshaw, John Porter, Henry Ramshead, Thomas Rigby, Robert M. Rigby, William Salthouse, Edward Snape.

In the Second World War, 8 more local lads fell: Thomas Allanson, Joseph Campbell, Norman Edwards, Michael Garner, James Thomas Garlick, Dennis Gregson, John Alfred Gillett, William Greenwood.

Since then, Keith V. Gardner (1959) and David Anthony Strickland (1982) have fallen whilst fighting for England and for those of us who remain. Let us not forget, and let us hope there are never any more names on there.

SERVICE REGISTER (X)

Qualifying Date 30th June, 1945.

**FYLDE PARLIAMENTARY DIVISION OF THE COUNTY OF LANCASTER
POLLING DISTRICT MM
FYLDE SOUTH ELECTORAL DIVISION**

Township of Bryning-with-Warton

Index Letters have the following meanings:— W—War Worker. S—Seaman.

L indicates Local Government Elector only.

Where no Index Letter is printed the elector is a Member of the Forces.

NOTE.—†Persons against whose names the mark † is placed are not entitled to vote in respect of that entry at Elections of County Councillors.
‡Persons against whose names the mark ‡ is placed are not entitled to vote in respect of that entry at Elections of Rural District Councillors.
§Persons against whose names the mark § is placed are not entitled to vote in respect of that entry in the case of a Borough, Metropolitan Borough or Urban District at Elections for Borough or District Councillors as the case may be and in the case of a Parish at Elections for Parish Councillors or at Parish Meetings.

15th October, 1945.

R. H. ADCOCK,
Electoral Registration Officer.

No.	Name (Surname first) Qualifying Address	No.	Name (Surname first) Qualifying Address
1	Appleyard, William, 20 Denwood Bank.	16	Parsons, Henry, 3 Harbour Avenue.
2	Barker, Roy, Rylands, Mill Lane.	17	Platt, Richard S., Branksome, Lytham Road.
3	Breckell, Henry, The Dene, Lytham Road.	18	Price, Richard, 2 Sunshine Villas, Lytham Road.
4	Davison, John, 6, Gracamy Avenue.	19	Rigby, Thomas, Wardley House, Church Road.
5	Dewhurst, Elise M., Bemersyde, Church Road.	20	Shelley, Albert, 1 West End Lane.
6	Dowbiggin, Maurice, Stanleigh, Lytham Road.	21	Sircom, Joan H., Runnymead, Church Road.
7	Eastham, Charlie, 6 Sunshine Villas, Lytham Road.	22	Smith, John J., School House, Lytham Road.
8	Fairhurst, Neville P., Thornhill, Lytham Road.	23	Townsend, Frederick, Moncrieff, Lytham Road.
9	Fenton, John, School House.	24	Townsend, Thomas, Oaklands, Church Road.
10	Haines, Malcolm W., Gould Dene, Lytham Road.	25	Tyson, Jack, Rose Dene.
11	Hankinson, Geoffrey F., Westfield, Guides Lane.	26	Unsworth, George W., 8 Harbour Avenue.
12	Ibison, John, Brentwood, Lytham Road.	27	Varley, Herbert, 2 Denwood Bank.
13	Lofts, Cecil G., 11 Denwood Bank.	28	Walker, Albert R., Clifton Arms Hotel.
14	Lofthouse, Henry R., Westbrook, Lytham Road.	29	Watson, Arthur, School House Bungalow.
15	Page, Arthur T., Hazeldene, Lytham Road.		

A later view of Warton Post Office. A telephone box has been installed and the sign over the door proclaims 'Public Telephone'. When alterations were made to the shop, the telephone box was moved nearer to the school and the bus timetable completely disapeared.

Mrs Ellen Townsend in the doorway of the original Post Office. The mail for Warton was addressed 'via Kirkham' where the mail cart that ran between Preston & Blackpool, arrived at 7.30am. The post was carried by a foot postman and was left at the smithy before the Post Office was opened in 1849. Ellen Townsend was postmistress for about sixty years, retiring at the age of 85. Two of her daughters, Elizabeth and Nellie took over.

(Mrs R Derbyshire)

E. Townsend,

GROCER and Tobacconist.

POST - - OFFICE, - WARTON.

Dealer in General House Requirements

Freckleton Parish Council Minute Book 23.3.1914

It was resolved unanimously that a letter be sent from the Ratepayers Meeting to the Postmaster at Preston with regard to the local postman having had his stripes taken from him, asking him to kindly reconsider his decision.

The Post Office with Mr Thomas Townsend and his daughter Ellen. The building is still recogniseable but a large shop window has been added. The main part of the shop is a grocers, but as in many village shops almost anything was available.

There are no spreading chestnut trees close enough to the District Bank, seen with its conical roof in this picture, but this is where the village smithy did stand until the bank replaced it in 1913. Can you hear the mighty roar of Freck's traffic? It is about 1930, there are no white or yellow lines on the road. No motor cars either, although the garage in the background caters for motorists. Just past the *'Coach & Horses'* on the left is a traffic sign telling motor drivers, and horse drivers too, that, because it had a trianglar top, they should exercise caution. It probably showed the flaming torch symbol to indicate *'SCHOOL AHEAD'*.

51

Two more views of Frecklton's city centre. In the upper view what was previously the *'Cyclists Arms'* has become a garage, probably William Rawstrone's, selling cycles and *'motor spirit'* (petrol). In the lower view we see the *'Coach and Horses'* on the right, we notice that electric light has come to town, and that the green has been fenced in. The photo was taken after 1927, when Preston New Road was built, and the *'finger post'* put up. The style, or lack of it, of the motor car suggests that the scene was captured in the 1930's

Kirkham Road Methodists.

Saturday was Kirkham Road Methodists' turn. About 200 sat down for tea. At the annual meeting in the evening the Rev. John Heaton was the speaker. Mr. Heaton is superintendent for a circuit which extends from Freckleton to Longridge, East to West, and from Ingle to Higher Walton, North to South.

A musical programme, consisting mainly of sacred music, was given by the church choir.

Mr. G. W. Rigby was the chairman. Nearly 83, Mr Rigby is the oldest member of the church trustees, and one to be proud of. He was about 20 years old when first appointed and has kept going ever since.

The present church, he told me, has been in existence 53 years next September. The previous one was on the same site.

"But really, going further back, Methodism in the village itself began at a farmhouse called Park Nook Farm. A house at Garston, six miles out of Liverpool, is called after the same place. The owner, Mr. Joseph Strickland, died nearly a fortnight ago, at the age of 83. He was a retired sergeant, and used to live near Park Nook Farm, and was very fond of it.

Looking towards Kirkham, we see here the Wesleyan Methodist Chapel on the left. Put up in 1884 to replace an 1840's chapel, it cost all of £1,400. The triangle-topped traffic sign warns of the cross-roads ahead, where Kirkham Road meets Lytham Road and Preston New Road at *'The Plough'*. This was long before today's traffic lights came on the scene.

Freckleton Rovers? United? Wednesday? Friday? We don't know the names of these 1920's teams, but we do know that John Threlfall, whose worldly goods these photos were, is on both. On the upper one · they've won a shield · he is on the goalie's immediate right, and on the other, possibly it was the village team, he is in the middle row, second in from the right. John went to Freckleton School, as undoubtedly did the two Rayton brothers (Ambrose & John) and Bill Iddon, also on the shield-winning team. Notice the uniformity of the shorts, the draw-string shirts, the leather, well-dubbined boots and the leather 'case ball'. Today's footballers know nowt.

(Mrs A Kay)

The three Tomlinson sisters on the farm, believed to be *'Further Hillock'* (From L to R) Alice, who became Mrs Harrison; Elizabeth who married a Bradley and moved to Wrea Green; and Ellen who has been mentioned before as Mrs Townsend, the Postmistress.

(Mrs R Derbyshire)

Some Freckleton lads and lasses. This group of church-going ladies are probably walking in procession through the town just after World War One, pushing a 'baby carriage', which was the common name for a 'perambulator'. (We call them 'prams', although even that word is going out of use). The tall lady pushing the carriage is Mrs Archer, wife of Jack. It is a study in fashion, as is the one of the frolic of Freckleton chaps out on the spree in Blackpool in the 1920's. Perhaps the two photos were taken on the same day!!! Six of the seven can be named:

Tip Bannister, ? in billycock hat, John Threlfall, John Rawstrone, Jim Swarbrick, Bill Iddon, Bill Sudell. Take note of their headgear, their casual cigarettes and the pleasure they felt at being on holiday for the day.

(Mrs A Kay)

A recent photo (ignore the 1950's Austin A.35 van under the verandah or *car port*) seen alongside one taken (much) earlier from the same spot. Until the 1880's, when all roads became council-owned, Preston (Old) Road was a turnpike, owned by a company who levied tolls for its use and erected houses alongside the tollgates put up to stop the paying road users. This one on the Preston-Lytham Road still stands, though the *'TOLLGATE'* sign has long gone. The bay windows allowed for vision either way along the road, letting the tollbooth keeper keep a look-out for customers.

(Mr R Hargreaves)

Warton's fund raisers meeting the challenge of *'Salute the Soldier Week'*. The organising committee with their guest of honour.

In the front row are Mrs Nellie Townsend, Mrs Ward, and Mrs Edna Braithwaite.

And in the second row are Mrs Ben Smith, Esme Fenton, Lena Swarbrick and May Kirby. Other locals include Mrs Janet Halstead, Mrs Grace Hankinson Snr. Peering over the officers' hats is Morris Braithwaite.

(Mr J Plummer)

Half the village turned out for the occasion. Lining the approach to the dais are Mrs Townsend, John Whittle, Barbara Proudlove, Ruth Benson, Peter Benson and (complete with collecting box ready to sell more flags). Isobel Atkinson

(Mr J Plummer)

Ladies and Gentlemen,

On May 8th, 1967, as ratepayers of this Parish of Bryning-with-Warton, you are asked to elect your representatives for the Fylde Rural District Council and the Parish Council of Bryning-with-Warton.

I have served the ratepayers of Warton on both these Councils, 27 years for the Parish and 15 years on the Fylde Rural District Council.

I have always taken an active part in the public life of the Village, and I ask for your support, in return I promise to do my best with my experience on both Councils.

Thank you.

Yours faithfully,

TOM TOWNSEND

Vote for . . .

T. TOWNSEND

Blacksmith's Shop. Warton

The old Blacksmiths shop next to the school. The site is marked today by an anvil on the forecourt of the garage. Owned by the Townsend family, the family business was started in 1906 by white-bearded Richard, seen here just a few years later with his son Thomas, grandsons John & Matthew. The little girl is Nellie, later the village Postmistress, and she is with her mother Ellen. John's son, Robert had a son, also Robert, who is currently running the business, and soon his son, another Robert, is joining the firm. Just for the record, the horse's name was 'Daisy Bell'

The road from Lytham in the 1930's. Brown's Farm, Warton is in the background. Taken when the road was being widened, the photograph shows a fine display of the tools of the trade.

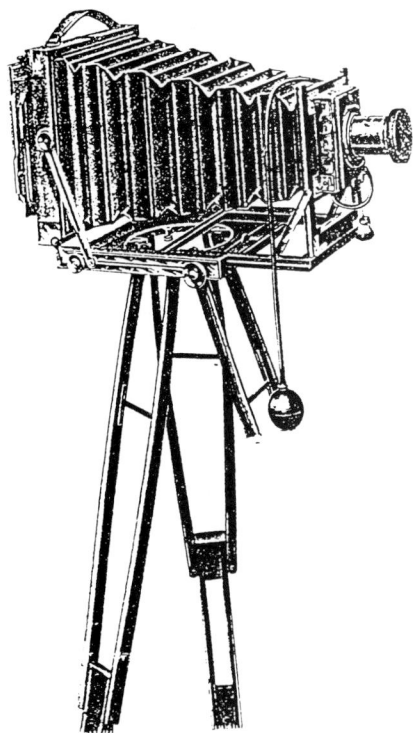

Coronation 1953. The village pensioners gather outside the school before going in for a meal and concert, organised by the Parish Council.

Councilor Morris Braithwaite, who was chairman of the council, is in the centre of the front row. Others included are Albert Smith, John Bonney, Bob Alkinson, Harry Bently, James Davison, Mrs Bickerstaffe, Mrs Britt, Ethel Coates, Maggie Bonney, Mrs Ward and Mrs Coates.

FRECKLETON PARISH ALLOTMENT HOLDERS 1914

List of the keepers of the council's allotments and the half year's in May 1914: Charles Whittle £1.2.6d; Robert Rawstrone 3s.6d; John Banks £1.5.10d; Thomas Banks £1.5.10d; William Cardwell £2.11.8d; T.H. Cardwell £1.0.11d; John Wilson £1.0.11d; James Porter £2.1.11d; T. Gavan Rawstrone £2.16.5d; George Bannister £2.16.5d; Thomas Banks £2.0.0d; John Wilson 5s; Henry Whiteside (two) £1.5.0d; & 5s; John Cardwell £1.15.3d; John Kirby £1.15.0d; Edward Hankinson £1.0.0d. Total Income £24.11.2d

Warton's Church is dedicated to St. Paul. This, the first one was built in 1724 (although Baines states 1722), as a Chapel of Ease to Kirkham. It was consecrated in 1725, but replaced in 1886 by the present one. The walls were lime washed cream coloured. The inside was noted as *'looking older than the outside'*. Across the western end there was a gallery where the organ was housed, with a door to the belfry.

The church held over three hundred people and the average attendance was stated to be over one hundred and fifty, in the 1870's

Reminder of the Fylde's darkest day - 23rd August 1944, when 61 people, including 38 children, died when an American Liberator bomber crashed on Freckleton School. It had been hit by lightning as it was returning to its Warton base. The memorial to those lost is in Holy Trinity Churchyard.

In a strange way, the word 'lightning' was to come to be associated with the area once again in the 1950's when the world- famous 'English Electric Lightning' fighter aircraft was to bring jobs to local folk as well as honour and security to this country.

The eighteenth of October 1961, and Mr Tom Townsend feeds his chickens while behind him the latest creation of the G.E.C Plastics factory is assembled to make sure the hundreds of triangular plastic panels all fit together. These structures are still used to protect radar aerials from the elements.
(Mrs R. Derbyshire)